MW01139928

theresa
all le Best

Losing my brotherhood

a collection of poems

Bobby Long

Copyright © 2012 Bobby Long
All Rights Reserved.

This book is copyright in all countries.

First Edition 2012

SGO MUSIC PUBLISHING LTD
PO Box 2015 Salisbury SP2 7WU UK
www.sgomusic.com

ABOUT THE AUTHOR

Bobby Long, from Wigan, England, is a songwriter and writer currently residing in New York City. He lives there with his girlfriend and cat Isis. This is his first book of poetry.

CREDITS

Illustrations by Ben Edge (www.theespivs.blogspot.com)

Edited by Sharon Weisz (w3publicrelations.com)

Cover Design by Tim McCarthy

Cover Photo: *Four Mennonite Farmers* by William Waldron (williamwaldron.com) Used by permission.

Back Cover Photo by Sharon Weisz

Editorial Advisor: Stuart Ongley (sgomusic.com)

Visit: www.bobbylong.info

For EDNA

CONTENTS

ILLUSTRATIONS

by Ben Edge

From The Start

Seeing it all right now

I see it all for the first time

like I was never here

that's why I keep coming

to replace myself with nothing

so that maybe

I can start again

First Attempt

Under some patchwork quilt that used to get used at the beach
you laid with me wondering if I would see you again.
As you turned on your side, some old sand fell
onto your naked arms
ironically showing me the swift fall of time
and your attention grew divided.
With both a record player and TV flickering and
playing in the background
a song I had never heard by a band that wouldn't matter,
I said this, and you said I was angry cause
you were leaving in an hour
and to just be still and enjoy this moment.
I tried to be still but your breathing engaged me to pursue
another moving line
that hid under your muffled drum of breathing.
I threw a few nice words out under the cover
in time with an old alarm clock that helped you drift
to sleep, and my words did the same,
you just went.
I seemed to think I knew everything about you,
you didn't know anything about me
you didn't need to

River Sister

the river flowed against my weeping leg scarred
like the memories you once gave me
the reed's coarse hairs split the tension and dread

always ending up here with the passing gives me hope
that things change and sometimes pass,
I just want to see my sister dancing

the ledge of the banks is my helping hand,
our grandfather carved them out with his spade,
he never wanted you in the deep sand

the restlessness of my nature is true,
especially here in mirrored nature,
you lean and grow with every planted yew

I'm cold and numb inside this young river,
and I'll meet you here soon come the summer,
you grow and I'll be the one to wither.

Me And Us In The Dark

you stopped the raid
torch in hand
breathing heavily
like someone who cared
some dress you slipped on
ruffled my feathers
who did it come from
I pretended not to know
I knew how the Indians felt
intruders at the shore
and now I was in trouble
a double dose of adrenaline
the other woman walked in
the lights turned on
I was alone
they both fled arm in arm
I was in the wrong room again
drunk in the dark

Happy Fucking Birthday

Come spill the birthday balloons

and blow out the candles

lick your lips and blow the frosting clean.

I tried to make today about you

and clean my mind of other things.

So I'll turn down the lights and we'll sing you a song

I'll run my fingers through your salon hair

and won't chip your new fingernails.

When the crowds retreat tonight

I will clear your path to your bed

and lay awake with you as you pull the safety clips

from around your cleavage

the brown wet wipes splurged with your makeup tissues

high in the bin

and your alcoholic breath on my cheek

To California

I heard she walks through the artist's workshop nightly,
Picking up the scraps fallen from the vice
It was there that they played my song on the radio,
Hoping she would recognize my humble voice.
Nothing that was ever created there
Could match all of her beauty and her way
I'm not aware they ever did see her
They never made work like that during the day.
She struggled like her nature did foresee,
And bounced between a job, a room and fame.
Men struggled to tie her down and woo her,
I whispered, Let her roam free and speak her name.
Following her down to California,
Still she scarred me like a claw and provoked blood
I left a plastic rose to age on her window sill
To remind her that real beauty never does.
The sun, it did nothing to shirk my love
It bowed my cracks and filled them in with lead
She let me carry her books home and saunter,
Still she would not let me take her to her bed.
Just to have the chance to hear her heart beat
Would be enough for me to retire and reflect

I can never hope to walk beside her,

For she walks too fast and I can't recollect.

I wrote a letter for all my heartache,

That expressed all that I would demand

Yet my words fell silent on a heart made of glass,

And I cursed the day that fire torched the sand.

Without a choice, I drank myself sober,

To understand the way that I'd been led

Then I moved out of her California,

Went home to my poor lady instead.

I often have the time to think about her,

Again to feel the whim of youth and tide

I hope she felt happiness before too long,

That something I just could not provide.

That something I just could not provide.

Losing My Brotherhood

Losing My Brotherhood

I lost my midnight call and sweep
my drugs and wet dregs
broken windows and stolen street signs
running from the police
through the AM streets cordially tied up with drunken whim
I lost my brotherhood

I lost my brother on the wall of my lost and found
As the autumn of youth washes over us and
mountains form around us
we're left to climb alone, tied to some craggy rock
in the hands of what's left
me and you, my swashbuckling tourniquet of my arm
I lost my brotherhood

Alone we step through the walked streets blinded by the street lights
outwalked by the cascading rigors we're holding
the bills we owe and the girls on our arms
keeping us upright
keeping us on the middle road
I lost my brotherhood when I left for the Americas

Like a lost Columbus and wooed by the song "Sail Away"
I lost my borrowed cigarette and second hand smoke,
I have lost my brotherhood

But I'm back to reclaim what's mine
in the misty memories of another claret spilled fight
Black-eyed and swollen fists
throwing out punches to knock out the heads
Losing my brotherhood

Phone Call

she chooses not to be with me
and excuses my calls
but I get calls from her at 3.30 AM
her trying to talk
and that's ok

Little One

A subtle blow to my head and the whimsical blood
pours off my brow,
As I'm helped to clamber to my feet
everyone knows of your way now,
You swap my passion for disdain and ponder at my every move,
You're a big girl now little one,
And I'll always have something to prove.

The anger you have is alight to those that
wouldn't dare to try and to taste,
Your armchair valor is once comforting,
but to a second it's really a waste.
How dare me try to look beyond and not think to look back,
You're a big girl now little one,
And you're starting to split and crack.

You can carry so much yet your carrion is
begging to wither and mold
I'm holding your sweet hands and
even I'm feeling my bones shrivel and fold
Here we are two bodies unable to move and think
You're a big girl now little one,
And it appears we're one for the sink.

Our house will always be empty although
we're still here trying to fill it,
Your head will always be full of regret though
you choose not to admit it,
These words they just keep ringing and quickly coming around
You're a big girl little one,
And soon things will come to rest on the ground.

I'm caught in the net that you cast and
I can neither find my way in or out,
I feel both a stranger to you and cautious
whether you whisper or shout,
Our integrity is real but our reasons are getting weak,
You're a big girl little one,
It's not who you are it's still what you seek.

So here we stand, you're empty,
you've invested your time in nothing but me,
After a flurry of words, you're still further than ever
from the word you call free,
Your flatulent flurry of insults has lacked the opulent strike
You're a little girl little one
And it's not what you know, it's who you dislike.

The Barricades

The Barricades

I felt the rustling leaves under my feet as we walked
through the barricades.
Someone shouted "the Russians are coming," and we grabbed
our sticks, and we pulled our weight with all our might.
Our ripped clothes and bloody knees wept, and we could
hear the dogs coming, chattering wildly on the cove.
Our lewd behavior on the Wiltshire moor,
our destruction on hay bales and corn fields was worth the victory
and mention in the papers.
We fought them in the trees and pilled and pillaged
like real men at war.
All of us on this small island are born fighters hastened to pull
the first blow or deflect the causes of recline
for more comes the battery when you retreat.
This is a fact embedded in the pillagers of yesterday,
for all to see in the libraries where we are forced to be seated.
See me and the boys carried into those fields,
the same thing that carried Mary to the inn,
the donkey of expectation,
the donkey that nature intended to carry Mary.
We had to fight because our fathers did, like that donkey
bore weight that its ancestors
did.
Still…..
We boys own that field and everything back towards our street.

Like guerrilla warfare, we hid and foraged from our parents
as the first injured made it back home.
A loose stick caught the arm of a young soldier and pierced his bicep
leaving yet more blood on that field.
No one made it home before nightfall, but places change
once the dark hits it,
and we happily handed it back over to nature once more.
We won't speak at school of the last battle and soon
we will be back, lurking in the hedgerow,
hiding from the fathers who gave this to us.

A Piece Lost

I lost a piece with your smell inside of it
I misplaced my most prized possession in a moment of me falling
But I still have the hem of your dress
the bit of your dress you ripped off to cover my fighting scar.
I promised you I wouldn't fight again
I have fulfilled that promise

The piece I lost was your old jewelry box
as you used to involve yourself in your perfume
the dregs would fall into the satin inlay of the box.
I don't care much for the box
just your smell inside of it

I actually hate that box
I hate the coils of metal and the opal plastic you call jewelry
all in all I am not a firm believer in you
but your odor, your smell
is what I need most

It reminds me of a time when we first met
two kids with nothing but a pure instinct
that smell resembles a time when we meant more to each other
when we worked together
I was the flower in your button hole
you were more to me than now
I was more to you than then

In A Glare

Beyond the groan of shimmer
the spectacular indecent murmur
of light behind your eyes,
bold and blue
like the oceans turning
crystallized in the wave of far content
I see your glare

The music springs forth from the cavern
the clink of glasses and the squeals of the girls
riding in the laps of some burly sailor
you in the water
far beyond any precipice
that I have with the noise and indecent current

You lay by yourself
feet to the air
like the champion whale
proud and unmatched
you're a daughter in the water
calming the sea birds

I turn and see the trail back to the house
is becoming darkened
it is time to leave

we are now beyond any glare that may wish to follow

but open to the night beasts

the birds and the crawlers

and you in the water

Them Dogs

Them Dogs

A shattering of light upon the hilltop
turns my gaze to the east to my lost home.
A pilfering storm,
to match my forlorn,
and the dogs are howling again.

The flower pots are empty and still,
the wind dials are turning like they have never turned.
The cold wind blows,
like there's something it knows,
and the dogs are howling again.

I see some faces twisted through marble glass in a nearby house,
they have lit their fires to strengthen their bones.
As the chimney side thickens,
the leaving smoke quickens,
and the dogs are howling again.

I walk alongside the dangerous road,
on the dangerous street somewhere beyond the dangerous town.
Here's where I'll be,
when they come looking for me,
until the dogs stop howling again.

My clothes are stained with oil,
the soil is dense with stones and winding weeds.

They say nothing here will grow,
but I don't think they know,
that the dogs are howling again.

I always wanted to be a pioneer,
somewhere headed to find space between heat and ice.
But if there is nothing to find,
since the world did unwind,
still the dogs are howling again.

Ballad for James Jucipher

He sings before her like a herald from the Bible
splitting into the quivers and undergarments of the women
rouge tone on his speaking bow
the history of him is for us all to see
but he wants to be set in stone

He was lost for years
thinking about the walls and opaque craters
the melancholic black skims his eyes shut
and the dew and honey cast him in stone
As he bows and bows
before and after
our eyes shut for just a moment too

A herald on the pulpit of this old theater
in this old theater we have seen one of Jehovah's gifts
he stresses and caves in his falling through the catacombs
she feels guilty for telling him she does not love him
he feels guilty that she will not love him
he does not want this gift
He wants her

The Lost Morning

The Lost Morning

The good part of the day is wrapped up inside a youthful morning,
the echoes of last night caught in the stones of our buildings
bouncing through the alleyways and hovels.
Its wind's dead but for the mild whip and dregs
from last night's storm.
Ideas fruitful and bound inside the energy that has congregated
since the night as one last straggler makes it inside.
The brightness from the sun peaking and rising above the trees
and outlines of the apartment buildings.
The dark still clings to the low places and cracks close to the floor.
The martyr gives himself to the morning and
scratches his legs before us,
the drunks squirm and squeal together ringing out their tongues.
The birds keep tune with the atoms in the wood,
the cab drivers end their shifts about to tag out.
I shuffle the lines of the road and dance to the workmen,
hammering and digging up the water pipes that
clean us in the morning.
I let in the rural pace that smacks my oblivion of sleep
with a needle to the eyes.
The lovers still count themselves lucky that they have each other
as he sees the beauty in her when she sleeps.
Softly and lazily laid out on their soft-sheeted bed

River Death

The river grew in size as the trees floated down like crocodiles,
15 feet of water covered gardens, it covered sun dials,
I saw a drowning dog clinging to the bank for a long time,
No one wanted to get their feet wet until the sun shined.

The factory had been pumping in sewage since 1952,
Then the tractors came and tried to make their own way through,
The driver lost his life getting swept up in that mess,
His wife fell to the ground as the rain ruined her dress.

Schools got evacuated and we all got sent home,
Wet feet and damp love with my friend Caroline,
My father helped put the sandbags up
as the river grew heavy at the core,
He said that come night time we'd have lost a few men more.

The electricity got switched off so we were candlelight,
Us and four other families staying warm holding the floodlight,
I saw a coffin in a boat, I saw a few more dragged by men,
My mother never thought she would see this again.

We called for help and lit fires but the phones were down,
No one saw the smoke, no one came around,
My father made it back wet and in tattered rag,
He saved our dog but he had to wrap and drag.

We made it out okay before the flood came over the barricade,
We don't know who we lost to that violent wave,
I hope Caroline got out with her mum and dad,
My father thought he saw them in the wake of the fad.

He slept well that night I watched over him until the sun came up,
He shivered out his fever, then my mother filled his cup,
He had to salvage what he could so we could leave our home,
The currents had us surrounded and the walls began to moan.

Things never went back, things will always change,
My family moved on up the hill and out of range,
We saw the droves of folk and damp refugees,
Once a proud people now like swarming fleas.

They sang songs about us, about that tractor in the dirt,
From digging crossways and trenches, and it made the river burst,
Then came the sleet rain as long as a mile and as heavy as stone
The dam couldn't hold it in, the sewage plundered all we had known.

The Things I Did And Do

I dropped some cigarette ash on your neatly cut hair

I made your morning coffee slightly cold

I wept at films that you deemed too bold

and pretended I didn't need subtitles.

These are the things I do to make you flinch

I played Bach at a higher speed on the record player

I pretended it was broken when you picked out Van Morrison

I sang harmonies to every line when you fixed it

and dragged my feet when you asked me to change sides.

This is what I do to annoy you

I poured Starbucks into your independent coffee store cup

I lied about my mother's age and said I was adopted

I read you Pablo Neruda when you picked out Frost

and changed the words around and made them all about summer.

This is what I do to confuse you

I never let you help me with the morning crossword

I went on walks for hours and didn't call

I drank myself into such rich stupors I couldn't stand

and lied about the trivial shit.

This is what I do because I am a bastard

I watch you sleep and block the morning light out of your eyes

I cook your favorite meal three nights a week

even though I'm allergic

I listen to your friends talk about their friends

I stopped going to the bar.

Just because

The Mores Of Social Distress

The Mores Of Social Distress

I'm entangled on the mores of social distress,
beyond the handshakes and plastic smiles of the business,
and the hawks of the legislation looking down.
The accountant's false friendship roping me like an old cowboy,
me the bull and my wife the cow.

Together we sit through the daily meetings
with blood being smeared up with windshield wipers
and tears used to lubricate the cogs.
I sit bound thinking of my youth
all a story now
amongst the pillars of this reckless regime.

With two hands on the necks of the young and dreaming
the stars are fading,
the wind is no longer blowing,
my dream is no longer dreaming.
My heart is beating harder than it has ever beat,
my veins are no longer mine,
they belong to the cogs and bald headed men.

I'm Sugar Ray Robinson,
on the ropes,
needing a knockout.
I'm the whitewash on the walls,
not noticed by society,

blemished with stains and crayon,

in the buildings of the cogs,

on the mores of social distress

Shanty Me Shanty

Lucid speaking through the oceans of our disconnect

I lost you on the rocks close to the shore

Lost to the deep and the willowed cave of the underneath

circled by the majesty sharks and torn in two

by the great white whale.

The rope tied to your body burning and pulling

your wet skin away from me

Send the anchor down to wedge me here close to where you may be

The frothy coma splashing and pulling me west and south

I'll pull the current over the town's eyes until you softly sleep

My secret in the tight confines of a glass bottle

My secret in the wreckage of the Amelia's lost plane and

the pits of the Fitzgerald with her crew

Seeing the other side and the sunset on the horizon,

I'll let it rock me to sleep to fight

another true day

Always the last day that you will be mine

Until tomorrow

And I'll take on the barren sea with a dark wind and

a sailor's intuition

throwing out the nets to the bottom

trying to catch your heart

For America

For America

In a barren room for two months,

where they walk the wooden floorboards,

he somehow escaped.

Fled at 4AM with the docile cave of his hunger,

he stole fruit and a bird basket for his journey, and

a jar of meat fat from a meek woman who took pity on him

and stuffed him into her laundry basket.

He killed the guard about to shed light on his moving position,

he thought of the children's faces and

his muscles tensed in fits of anger and desperation.

Now he would find his own family and, hopefully, alive.

Far enough away he rested under a low bridge,

he dreamed they were hiding in the shadows

covered under potato sacks,

tacked together with clothes pegs like he taught them not so long ago.

His mother and father were there also,

although his father was old,

he bore the strength of a young man and

would take out at least two should he need to.

In his dreams he sensed the soldiers near by and

the lights brushed the shadows,

like stunned rabbits the children froze and

clenched there hands blood dry.

His father held his knife at the ready,

the soldiers soon passed,

he awoke from the deep frightful slumber,

sweating and time to move on.
He would find a way home soon
and leave for America.

Essex Street Crawl

The wind switches patterns down Essex Street,
comforting to some yet unhinged and merry
to the late night crawlers.
Micky picks up his bag and stumbles from
the close confines of the bar
his feet scuffling and nearly falling beneath him,
his bag open and losing its contents.
The rural sun is nearly on his trail and
the non-sleeper in 166 is losing his mind
Essex Street is alive again
too late for some,
and too early for others.

Horror On Clinton Street

street jumper

suicide hopeful

legs dangling

crowds underneath parted for the splatter

police sirens off not to distract her attention

gasp and shock, mouths covered as she slips

she reaches out to the help and clings on by a thumb

they drag her back to the roof

kicking and screaming the night away

applause dawns the street

a street man steals from an open cotton pocket

friend of the jumper

"do they do this as a scam"

"does he make her pretend to jump"

I hope so

free theater on Clinton Street

from horror to a crime play

in half a jump

Just Like Hollywood

below the weaves of people on Avenue A

some granite block

some imprinted hand

with a name carved in it

just like Hollywood

like her

to me

Man – Hattan

deep in Manhattan lies a deeper meaning
everybody knows it's not something you speak of
it's not a cluster of dreams you dream of
for all the gifts you have ever spat on
will pull you closer to your right wrong
In Man-hattan

Looking Out

A porcelain doll's head resting against the wooden burrow
a set of keys hung up next to the dry dead flowers
odorless and crinkled in the moving sun
Central Park in the distance.
Horse-drawn history teachers carrying the pilgrims
film sets follow old trees, follow the park's hawk
kids clinging to the blanket, mother on the hand rail.
Lennon's shot dead there every day,
Culkin is shown the door,
beads are traded and locals move away.
Back in the room where the memory is fading fast
where my imagination is roaming free
in the sterile ink and botched typewriter
in the cracked screen of a laptop.
Looking through the wall of daydreams
and into the misspent times of yesterday
flocks of geese trail the smoke of the aircraft
flocks of people trail the sun-drenched side of the street.
I trail the moving hordes to the end of Central Park
to the roof of the Dakota and a lit candle for Lennon
I think I can see Washington Square
I think I can make out faces of the people I have met or known
on holiday from England
this enables my will to stay inside
in the confines of dead flowers and hung keys
and a moving sun.

The Day We Go Home

If this is the right time
things will all fall in line
tightly knit with twine
if this is the right time

If this is the wrong place
we will leave without a trace
and move this fabricated space
if this is the wrong place

If we hear the wrong word
we will think it's all absurd
and pretend we never heard
if we hear the wrong word

If we seem it fit to run
I will sound the starting gun
I promise under the sun
if we seem it fit to run

If the forces deem me unfit
I will forage, I will outwit
I will show you my true grit
if they deem me to be unfit

If they come knocking at our door
I will pull them to the floor
and not give them chance for kind report
if they come knocking at our door

If I ever turn on you
with ever nail and brush I clamber through
though it's something I will never do
I will never turn on you

But if you ever want rid of me
I will divert them and I will flee
for you to run and be free
if they ever want rid of me

This is time for you to go
don't speak a word for I already know
with every action that you show
this is time for you to go

If I go before my time
I will see you down the line
for you me and mine
if I go before my time

No More, No More

No more running from the wolves
No more time spent in your arms
No more edge of the sword
I'll be back when you're wrong.

No more traveler's foot and cramp
No more hiding from the spirits
No more edge of the water
I'll be back when you're wrong.

No more chances wasted and spurned
No more need for victory
No more rights to wrong
I'll be back when you're wrong.

No more beacons lifted and lit
No more glasses on the bar
No more friends to lose and gain
I'll be back when you're wrong.

No more places I have been
No more lights to blind my eyes
No more tales that I have told
I'll be back when you're wrong.

No more reels and no more wire
No more songs to play your ears
No more restless night's sleep
I'll be back when you're wrong.

No more digging of the grave
No more hands baying for my blood
And no more blood drawn from the stone
I'll be back when you're wrong.

No more clashing of shields
Please lay my shield upon the ground
No more birds up in that sky
I'll be back when you're wrong.

No more roadside stop
No more roadkill on that road
No more sweat turned to salt
I'll be back when you're wrong.

Waiting For The Call

It's these winding hills
that split my mind,
it's these innocent crooks and open crevices
that bring me closer to the middle,
it's the morning dew that waters the earth
and freshens my dry mouth,
come nature the natural clock.
Let's wind up the sun and crescent moon,
the calls at night that scare my mother
some nightbird living its day,
and the creaking of the morning.
Its scattered cloak
filling those crevices and crooks,
the ones I hide in
when I think of home.
The dusty cloak of my youth
beaten to retrieve memories,
it will all just fall to the earth
and there the cycle begins.
On its footpaths
centuries old
walked by my fathers,
now those old pipes are exposed
a new home for something small.
The English seasons
driving rain

lasting light of summer
and uncut frost scattered on tree and cement,
still they hold my needs
and I'll come hold them again.

We Are Gonna Fall Under Our Weight

We are gonna fall under the weight of ourselves
under the cryptic genetic system that once rose us up.
Under the sheer bones and mass of our bodies
to explore technology, film and the arts
we will fall upon ourselves.
Then we will be lynched to hate ourselves
like God intended.
The mysterious God that flickers through my system and
gives me hope
or the reasons for any fortune.
We will fall under the hopeless romantics that we truly are.
The arts will fold and become benign,
the political system will corrupt itself straight
but we will not be there to witness it.
We will be under the full weight of our bodies,
writhing in mystery,
writhing in confusion,
and sunk back to Earth.

Romance On The Road

if you need me

my broken down car

the one your father drove too far

I promise to be earnest and sweet

and carry you to ease your wounded feet

I Would Like To Think That

I Would Like To Think That

Strolling the alleys that come night is beyond me
or so you say,
I would like to think that you're sometimes right
and so I'll believe you

My poverty revealed by my wet feet
on this wet street with this wet rain,
I would like to think that maybe some time
you would carry me

Though I won't deny that I don't like the flesh,
you may pretend, I know you used to,
I would like to think that maybe soon
we can talk about that

Ducking into some Stanton Street shop for cover
pretending to purchase or to be out of breath,
I would like to think that I always am
and they believe me

The misshapen pavements or broken sidewalks
filled up and drained out,
I would like to think that
they hold something, sometimes

and I would like to think that some things are,

because they are

One For The Millions

The Falling Grace,
the whimsical fall from God
clearing the ground and moving the moved
seeding the seeds
and pollinating the pollen.
On this great day
when nothing will come to worry
not even the crude sirens
and bums asking for money.
Somehow they're feeding themselves
and the sirens are not for ringing
for someone accidentally flicked a switch
all in all
like Lou Reed said
A perfect day

A Hero's Wedding

I'll be your bride and groom
your veil and garter
holding you up when you're on show
your something borrowed when you're blue
your drunken uncle when you've had a few
your distant cousins and old school friends
some babbling minister talking about sex
unconventional and hip
coughing through that uncomfortable moment
your mother crying
a father's speech
your hungover brother holding back the puke
I'm your working class
when you fall upon it
your upper class
when you feel like rising up
your bridesmaids trying to sleep with the best man
that one guest always wearing white
the tea and buffet
your leftover thin cut salmon
I'm filling empty stomachs and weary heads
I'm your foreign affair but I won't turn up
the person who pays for the band
the distant divorce
that last happy dance

I'll call the taxi cabs and drive the drunk home

I checked them in at the front desk

little sister is sick and grandma has been sleeping for 3 hours

but I lost the ring

I lost you

I arrived late

and you're the one getting married

If I Saw Leonard Cohen

If I saw Leonard Cohen
I would bow my hat and take a knee
And at the same time grab his hand to my heart
And remind him though his youth is fading he has mine
When the time is right I'll write for him
Like Salieri did for Mozart
Without the trek of deceit and jealousy
To note down anything that would drip from
the tap of his subconscious
Anything that would spill from his cup of knowledge
To write down about the last holiday with Suzanne
The reunion with Marianne
And the last battle of the partisans
I would remind him that everybody still knows
that Manhattan and Berlin are both slowly falling

Still the future is a bruised bleeding mess
though the blade has departed
the trail to its fleeting is still in sight
to tell him that I still read from that book of longing
and never have I had more will
to be the traitor

I will go out and collect the meat sandwiches
and light the candles
sincerely yours

The Pulpit

Speak your words
to the whites and blacks
to the men and women
and girls and boys.
Speak your words
to poker brand the young and old
and flurry those left in the middle
with the underline.

Fight To The Death

Fight To The Death

Inside this courtyard
me and my friend
the one who shot me dead
never has nature seen a crueler blow
than the one he gave to me

I thought that it would always be us
surrounded by this debacle
the chimes of our youth in sync
our parents were friends
until I told them what he did

Bloody autumn
leaves fell like the punches on the back of my head
my friend slugging like Judas
dancing for the year above
tears dropped like my body to the floor
one for every time I helped him

A year later he was thirsty
an hour of miserable cross country
he turned to me for help
I drank the bottle in front of him
some old wound I guess

Yet when all were on him,

he fought three guys on the school field

it was me who put out a leg to trip up one

he didn't see

but he saw me on his way home

As these years fall around us now

I've moved away

he sits around at home

with his old school girlfriend, diets and Pampers

I threw his apology from the window

So inside this courtyard

me and my old friend

I won't turn my back

to this lumbering spirit

that wants again to be my friend

Jerusalem

In the castle of my heart,
In the loose cold tomb of Richard,
On the handle of his gallant sword,
Pilfering and pillaging the passion.
Into the vestibule of my mind,
Into the dormant cluster of Guinevere.
The dress of my thoughts,
The traitors flaunt for my best friend.
Into the Lancelot of my soul,
The solo spoiler and battling fighter.
In the battle and close to tormenting myself,
Close to an end and close to the start.

The Trier

The Trier

every street holds its twisted sign
just like you hold my twisted hand
your path is the road which I stand on
and your way is its fleeting light

I look at you and I'm reminded of the short cusp of time
the guillotine that swings above me
I look at you and you disappear
like the falling dust in my mind's eye
I have to track your outskirts
otherwise you disappear into nothing
like you were never here

in all that you do
you seem to handle everything without consequence or passion
because trying is enough
I watch you try and that's enough for me
everyone thinks so
you're the trier
you're the one everyone laughs with
when you come in last place
they carry you off the field because you're an artist
like some homecoming queen on stilts

when you hold my twisted hand
I feel you wash over me
just that one time I'm held aloft
please don't stop trying to try with me
I'll be your twisted sign on your well-lit road
I can't help but try

Baby In The Water

I heard about your militia
I heard about your history
And yet you still believe in what you're saying?
Or what they spoke about?
I heard about your Bible
I held your old Koran
and yet you still follow those poor men?

I have a baby in the bath
who needs bathing
she speaks to me sometimes
she is my golden goddess
and does not speak of any of these things to me.

What I Done

I saw the spear that struck Jesus with his final blow
the blow that plants guilt and sacrifice on us all.
I have the end of the cigar lit when Winston Churchill gave his speech,
it still smells of victory, and I relight it occasionally
on Sunday evenings.
I held the microphone to the lips of Martin Luther King
and passed him a white tissue for his proud brow.
I leashed the lion that Saint Jerome helped,
I have the thorn on my bedside table.
I held the red rose of the Lancastrians during the War of the Roses,
not until the white rose fell did I relinquish.
I pressed the button that dropped the "ungodly" bomb
on the poor people of Hiroshima,
I was forced and I regret daily.
I stood alongside the bill for gay marriage and condemned Diaz,
the ignorant bastard, for lack of equality.
I was beside Florence Nightingale and basked in the light
as she visited sick soldiers.
I stood over the body of Richard the Lion Heart and
carved the Round Table.
I served Frank Sinatra and Frank McCourt whiskey
in two separate bars,
I drank whiskey on my own in that bar and heard Nina Simone
perform "Strange Fruit" for the first time.

I flew a Lancaster Bomber
and watched the bombs drop into the ocean
on the border of Germany.
I leaned against the sweet drenched walls of the Cavern
and watched the Beatles perform "I Wanna Hold Your Hand"

What You Done

Us and Them (The contagious three)

So please let's have a few to drink
Let's stop the rot and bottomless sink
for all this confusion is making me think
and I tend to fall when I'm stood at the brink

so speak kindly to those who speak well of me
so often they choose to wander and flee
if they choose to sit under this vast oak tree
us and them the contagious three

the pot it boils heavy with its tale of woe
but life is hard for those who distinctly know
that the need to speak faster often brings the need to speak slow
please call our fathers if we decide to go

these rivers and roads are ours if we leave
let's earn our patronage and not fix to thieve
if we lose ourselves then we cannot retrieve
then what hope do we have to honestly breathe

then soon the clash will begin in your head
and the iron claw will not relinquish from your bed
stapled to your name and trail you when you're dead
for in history it's not what you see but what you have read

let's put together all that we have got

though this wood is strong its loins will rot

we will live and brew in our gardenia's lot

sometimes it's easier to have what we have not

the clutch that us binds is worth all that we are trying

some rain may be tears but it's not me crying

even come the day when people are dying

I was looked in the eye and never found lying

loose and churned like the salt of the earth

as loud and as pale as the day my mother gave birth

with four bags of lorries and enough self-worth

I'll be buried here under our well-kept turf

You're No Anne Boleyn

the clinical proposition of your clerical vision

your eyes are on me now

your eyes are on me now

you're wanting description of its made up fiction

and I don't know how you'll pull this back at all

your diluted rage to turn your other page

it's woeful and a lie

it's woeful and a lie

the subdued enclosure of your famous disclosure

has me covering up the bits that you forgot

the fanatical reprieve of all the people you deceive

the rumor's hit the road

the rumor's hit the road

another noise to ignore when the wind has stormed its floor

I won't cower and pretend it all again

so scream your denials from our country you defiled

you're no Anne Boleyn

you're no Anne Boleyn

if someone required your seduction I'd call it an abduction

somewhere between a hard place and a flame

nothing more deceiving is the incision of your feeling

like blood from the stone

like blood from the stone

you have no cryptic message for it's heralded by your presage

as open as a copied reading book

so lay your head upon the block for that person you forgot

it's time to play your game

it's time to play your game

You speak of wanting valor in this tried and tested hour

darling you will never be my Anne Boleyn

Fighting A Fight

Fighting A Fight

The ancient spindly line adept to creeping hordes
Activists and the like.
A cradling branch holding the lurching bundle and
the bird's homemade box.
The tentative stones holding court underneath yet
another unwilling siren,
driven for territory like the generals on battlefields of old.
A flash in the pan and still the rain falls like old times
Nothing here is making inroads.
Stuck within the problems and pages of another history book
Rain fills ditches and trenches on some man's plantation
Not willing for this fight.
These trees curved on the side of the hills like fans lingering over
the side of bleachers trying to retrieve a bad ground ball
in a passing moment I still saw the heat in the eyes of a white man.
There in another battlefield thought to be closed
the bird's looking down on them
the stone's underneath
There in the middle
Fighting a fight

Danish Brood

The Danish sea rumbled through the deep
and we held each other tight in the wind
I dreamt of my ancestors
the Viking brood roaring into the wind
mouth of salt
and chapped lips

I cowered in my seat
and my teeth chattered wildly
so much has been lost
in the long ropes and boats
and in the genes

On The Junk

I do not feel welcome
in your arms I sunk
I do not fret though
when you're on the junk,
your sapphire doldrums
you used to call for eyes
are all I really wanted
and all that I despise,
undone and untied slowly
like the very last bit of string
is your way and all you show me,
but still no alarms will ring

Sleepers Creepers

Cracked eyelids let the light in
Coarse pillow like wet chalk
And all the words I never wrote again

Cat's up whining and mauling her toy
Dog outside has found a friend
The girl next to me has run a fever

Some building fell down a few blocks up
A travesty on the radio in Colombia
And all without the new day

The neighbors are up stampeding cattle
The elephant has joined them
Someone should check the gas in the building

All the books I have never read or tried
Last night's food has burned me empty
Political riots steal my single vote

All in my head the Civil War
UFOs and burning crosses the last hanging
Blacks Whites and Mexicans falling out

I haven't been home for a year
My Mom's hair is grey
My friends are still getting married

I have to be up in an hour
Do I get up now or when my alarm goes off
I don't think I'm gonna feel any worse

I've counted higher than I ever have before
I have pulled apart the Lord's Prayer
I don't know when religion escaped me

My landlord is doing the rounds
He wears multi-colored hoodies and eats nuts
He rides a fucking fold-up bike

It's cold in here like it is outside
I'm reading John Cooper Clarke
I can't fucking sleep

The Mother's Wait

There is a woman on my street
wearing a shawl
she is sat out in any old chill
and is burnt by the sun
is thin and unwinding
she is waiting for her child
to take his place back in the house
there is much to do
and grass to be cut
and she has much to tell him

We don't know where he is
and he's been gone for a long time
maybe at war, abducted, maybe the needle
another vice of man's invention
another reason for man to hurt the woman

the mother's wait
that's what she is doing
waiting for man
the proud woman in a shawl

The Summer's Heat

The concise spear of summer,

penetrating the hordes of the beach and then

spurning time like children.

Red skin, blistered and scorn with the tides of the tide, tides of ray,

Mother laid out like grandma in her armchair.

Father with his belly carries arms of the bad child from the sea,

the board trailing in the sand,

done checking wet sand in little sister's eyes.

Essence of coconut and smoke and beer breath,

the shark warning caught in the shark net,

don't go out too far,

the summer's heat melting our eyes and holding in the memories.

The Wave Runners

They spread themselves out in lines against the beachy head
as winters turned to summers and I watched from the spring.
I buried my feet in the sand to regain my position and
standing as I threw stones into the overflowing bin.
The leaders tossed their blankets onto the sand and
ran off into the sea.
The wave pushed them back as the opal surf crushed and
scarred the backs of the young wave runners.
The miners of the wave rode the indecent stream
as it pillared the calm and cool waters beneath
before showing the teeth of its crest.
Snarling, bad tempered and too heavy to overrun
the boys were swept up and thrown to the deep.
Into the deep dear boys, into the deep.
Into the deep I heard them cry.

Mother's Tears

The dry Texas sky layered with red steps down to the ground,
the scope of endless years.
History in every bit of rain that falls down onto our heads.
The cascades and cross on top of the church that
still holds its sacrifice high,
none more in the weeping of mother's tears.
The poor old farmer, sweat glistens on his head and falls to his ground,
churned and soon to be planted with father's sacrifice.
The cross above shows the death of a man, far, far away
but these seeds get planted for the boys at home.
As does the dry sky of Texas, with its red steps up to the sky,
hold court over this land.

Trouble on the Ridge

Trouble on the Ridge

Upon this ridge that the moss is growing from
upon this ridge where it all fell silent.
curated by the night sky and let in by the wall of fog,
someone stood tall amongst the trees that you gave me.
This is your land my father
why don't you take it back,
and stay behind.

My grandfathers planted these trees on the ridge that we stand upon,
with my father in the pram and my mother in his heart.
So clear the moss and reveal the etchings,
reveal something you didn't know about me,
my grandmother cut her hand on this rock,
scrubbing my clothes.

Since then the river has dried up and grandma has passed,
the stone is like marble with the cutaway finish.
The trees have grown tall and have blocked out half the sky,
the birds have nested and moved on,
I still come back here to remind myself,
that upon this ridge where the moss grows,
the moss is still growing.

Until We Grow

Until We Grow

I saw a man draped in chains
speaking his name again and again
making it home from some forgotten hell
where the blood curdled cries come like the hourly bell

his name was muffled by his wounds
I wished someone had the nerve to write it down
that was all awhile ago from where we are now
still the sweat glistens for us all from his bloody brow

he told us his friends would be falling near
so we should cipher our distress when they come around
for they had been through enough of people turning their heads
that they didn't want answers just the warmth of their beds

in with the fog and out like the fad
a trembling distant rupture had been enforced
whipped like the dog but brave as your one true friend
some time soon we and them would feel the end

on this island no thing is buried, nothing shines
especially for that man draped in chains
the coldest breath of spring will surely know
just how much beauty we see until we grow
until we grow

To Break My Own

Adoring the pulpits of the characters around her,
swaying in the low heat that engulfs her low dress,
she takes her time.
She leans into the ears of the adoring and whispers into their ears,
the sun beats down on all of us but not on her,
not onto her skin.
The golden web of her dress erupts the dust under her feet,
the rolls of her hair fall down her back like Niagara,
as we take our seats in the modern coliseum.
Come the trumpets and drums and come forth the notes of the heat,
we sway beneath them under the frequencies
that dictate our movements,
her soft touch upon our eyes.
The horns ring out in triumphant nostalgia to
remind us of a time that was once gone,
and loose bells clang and ring.
I intentionally look at her and she looks at me,
I smile and she smiles,
A look to berate the hearts of men,
A look to break my own.

The Loose Cannon

A loose cannon of your hair recaptured my mind.

The whimsical fall of embedded amber, tousled and prime.

The swell of pity that echoes in my mind drags me through the dirt.

Tomorrow you may only be a will or a wish

but you know you're on my mind.

Say hello to me in mime or spell me out in those chemical drinks

you down before you throw in to the gym.

Will you escort me home with your sweating pallets,

drenched in envy.

My envy will dry you like the towel that hangs from your ragged bag.

Impenetrable Love

I used to be your favorite dead end street
until they knocked through the wall
I used to be your man
not so long ago.

I remember us both hushed lovers
fully clothed and only hands touching
getting home and listening to the green album
eating fruit gums and me spitting out chew
like a cowboy

I used to be your go-to man
for a bit of sensitivity around other 12-year-old boys
it was how I stood out to you
I would only ask you to wear your hair down
up you reminded me of our teachers
and school

I used to sit next to you in science and
whittled our names to the table leg
using left-handed, children's safety scissors
it took me all winter
The scavengers soon covered it with gum
as sticky and impenetrable as my feelings for you

I'll Be The Fisherman

I'll be the fishermen
seeped in the water
mingling with the fishes
and bait for the hungry

but if you let me go
I'll go down with the crowd
I will drown with the sailors
and rot with the shipwreck.

Diamond Daughter

She has opened her prism as her smoke drifts through the night.
A mother's daughter dressed like a string-a-long
a children's wound up toy.
Her heaven in clusters with all she has on the floor,
my diamond daughter, my innocent one,
My lukewarm gentle and still water,
weathering yet again,
another sea storm.

Let's Talk

Silent and slow
behind the tide
selfish for bruising
bruising for the selfishness
children's issues that never left

Let it out
and be my friend

On A Good Day

On A Good Day

I see the fifteen trees in the garden and see every branch
as a stage in a man's life.
Long at the bottom and growing shorter as it grows up,
and although the lengths are shorter
they hold more flowers and fruit.
The birds roost at the top and are less inclined
to the wind and stones.
We're all heading for the top.
When I'm alone in paradise I get the call from my friend and
they can see the loneliness in my head.
I'm the bird building the nest and
the hunter learning to refrain with his gun.
I'm happy to sit in the sand and carry
the alienated fish back to the surf.
I'm the comfortable passerby, and I'll make my home
out of clothes and a different wind.
I see my sisters smiling like the little girls they still are.
I empty my pockets to the homeless man with his dog and realize
I'm one bad mistake away from the street.
I stay clear of the bars and alleyways and keep the moon
close to my heart but not my heart in the dark.
A flowered dress can never lead to unhappiness.
Money is just a fool's way of deciphering apart from other fools and
it only leads to a misty perception.
A woman's love can cause a man to spill his every flaw.
Coffee and cigarettes lead me to happiness.

On a Bad Day

I'm a leftover, an open clam, a fish on his belly
just meters from the wave.
I'm a lone diner, a friend without friends and a rootless tree.
I'm the branch that's trailing at the foot of the trunk
looking up to his fruitful brothers.
I'm the one to be bitten by the snake when many believe that
they have all been driven from Ireland and
I'm the full proof sham that gets found out
and then thrown to the public.
I'm a foreign traveler who has lost his money and the damaged
binding holding all the pages in place of his void passport.
I'm the null tone and the pointlessness of the Queen's speech
at Christmas.
I am a leftover tree trunk in a forest
ruptured with fire (I am that fire),
as useful as a ready-made chocolate bird's nest.
I'm the dud wave in a surfer's paradise and
I'm a broken match in a soggy box of matches.
I'm the floor when all the seats have been taken and
the cut coil in your children's Slinky.
I am a bankrupt bank and a moldy pear well past its sell-by date.
I am the orphan child adopted by child smugglers and
your favorite Dickens novel unreadable in Arabic.
I am the fungus that has crusted itself on the skin of fresh milk and
the borrowed film that will never be returned.

I am your box of Christmas decorations in May and
a child's crayon mark
on the ceiling of the Sistine Chapel.

Peace in Silence

Ring the bell

Ring the silent bell

Until the people see and they can tell,

Not everything bold needs to make a sound

For if the lights are out

And the hunting hound,

Can see the path

And ease you in

Then darkness becomes a very small thing,

Like the hound, silence can bring you near

To all you wanted,

And make things clear.

Man for the People

Sleeping awake through the devout cynicism and
apathy that holds me today.
Un-rested and un-sweetened you cannot cling to the cliff anymore,
this way that I am.
I have had the very tops of my fingers chopped off
by the tyrant Fred West.
I'm a deep and structural myeloid mess where I can no more
offer myself the words of books and the words of wisdom.
Maybe I need my father or the whim of a pretty girl's hair
as it's all misty and bitter today,
out in the world.

I do not know a time or see a place that's fit for me anywhere.
Or anywhere that hides my time and place.
I shall move from land to sea and roam the cortical miles,
until home figures out
where I can escape from and call my heart.
No face is going to be a redeeming feature for me until
all twisted like an old harbor rope, soiled with oil
from the cigarettes that poison me.
I want to be the man for the people.
A man for the laughs and technology that form the roof
over our lucid bodies.
A man for the people I am.

ACKNOWLEDGEMENTS

The author wishes to thank the following ...

Stuart Ongley and his family

Nikki and her family

Sharon Weisz at W3

Brother Ben Edge

Martha North, True MGMT

William Waldron

Tim McCarthy

Teacher Mrs. Mills

Jon and Kev

and my family and friends

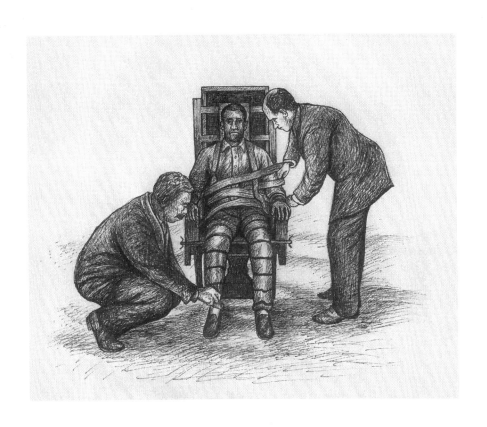

INDEX OF TITLES

15510031R00067

Made in the USA
Lexington, KY
01 June 2012